Kirstine Niko
Inge Lise Nik

Tatted

Handkerchiefs

Akacia

Previously by the same writers:

The DMC Book of Charted Tatting
(published in Danish with the title
Orkis - Forlaget Notabene)

Tatting - Just knots

The 3rd Tatting Book

Forlaget Akacia
Skovvænget 1
DK - 5690 Tommerup
akacia@akacia.dk

Printed at Øko-Tryk I/S, Videbæk, Denmark, 2002

ISBN: 87-7847-053-6

Introduction

The handkerchief became known in the Middle Ages. In the Middle Ages as well as in the Renaissance the handkerchief obtained a decorative function and these decorative handkerchiefs were embroidered with pearls and gold.

Today the paper tissue has replaced the handkerchief made of fabric but the decorative handkerchief with embroidery and laces is still used.

Tatting is very suitable for making lace and we have composed 12 patterns, all of them with corners, in the classical style.

We have mounted the laces on thin, white fabric - and created traditional decorative handkerchiefs - but the patterns are also suitable for a lot of other things such as napkins, doilies or christening robes.

Don't forget - the possibilities are innumerable for using tatting.

We hope you will enjoy the book.

Tommerup, Denmark
February 2002.

Explanation of symbols

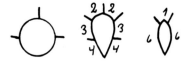

= Picots for joining or ornamentation. The figures are the number of double stitches

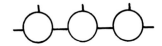

= Joining of picots in the same round

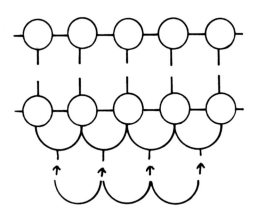

= Joining of rounds (picots pointing at each other)

= The arrows mark where to join the chains

= A B C D E succession of rings. a b c d e succession of chains

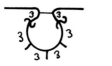 = Exchange shuttles at ~

 = Josephine knot

 = Split ring

 = Place to put in a paper clip either at the start of the work or to make an interval between the stitches

To join a chain to a handkerchief

The thread is pulled through a hole in the edge of the handkerchief with the help of a crochet hook.

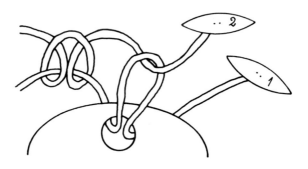

Lace No. 1

1 shuttle + ball thread.

Thread no. 80.

The lace is tatted in one round with 5 double stitches between each picot.

When the lace is finished, sew it to a piece of fine linen with a hemstitch.

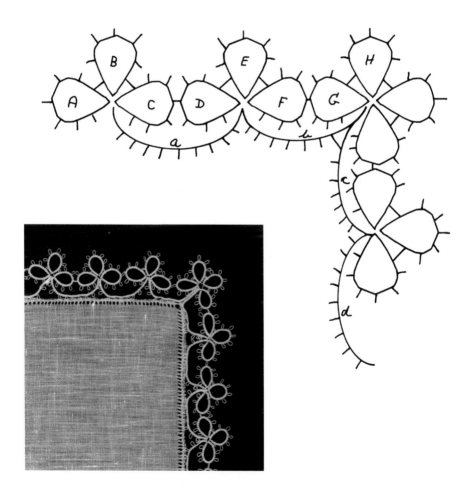

Lace No. 2

2 shuttles.
Thread no. 80.
Tatted in one round with 4 double stitches between each picot.
Remember to exchange shuttles at ~.
Sew the lace to a piece of fine linen with blanket stitches.

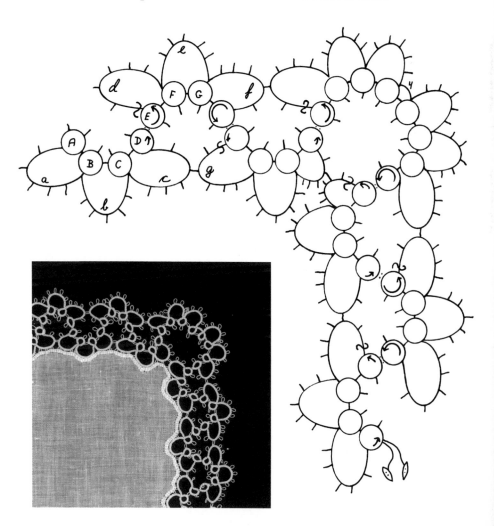

Lace No. 3

2 shuttles.
Thread no. 80
Tatted in one round.
Sew the lace to a piece of fine linen with a hemstitch.

Lace No. 4

2 shuttles. Thread no. 80.
Tatted in four rounds. The three outer rounds are made without cutting the thread. The innermost round is tatted at the end. Round one starts at A, then follow the alphabet. The second round starts with ring 1, then follow the series of numbers the opposite way around. The third round starts at ring 34. Make the innermost round in split rings at the end.
Sew the lace to a piece of fine linen with a hemstitch.

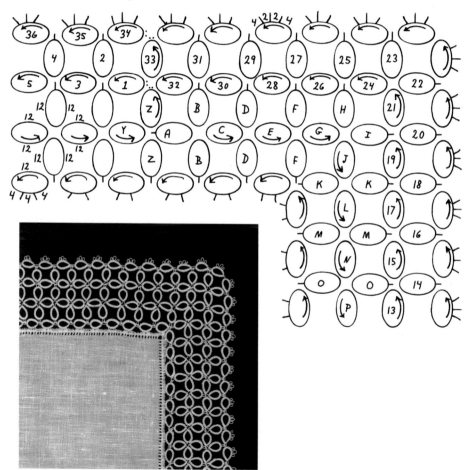

Lace No. 5

2 shuttles. Thread no. 80.

First tat and join the four flowers. Tat the chains around the flowers and join the work to the handkerchief. Complete the corner with a round of split rings and finally tat the lace around the handkerchief.

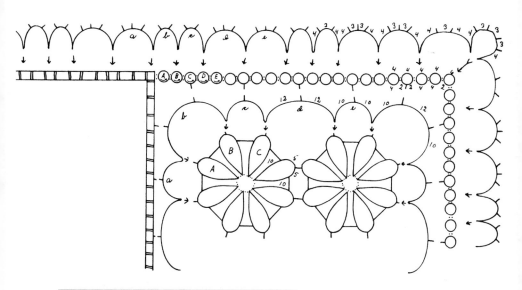

Lace No. 6

2 shuttles.
Thread no. 80.
Tatted in 2 rounds. First tat the innermost round onto the handkerchief, start with chain a.

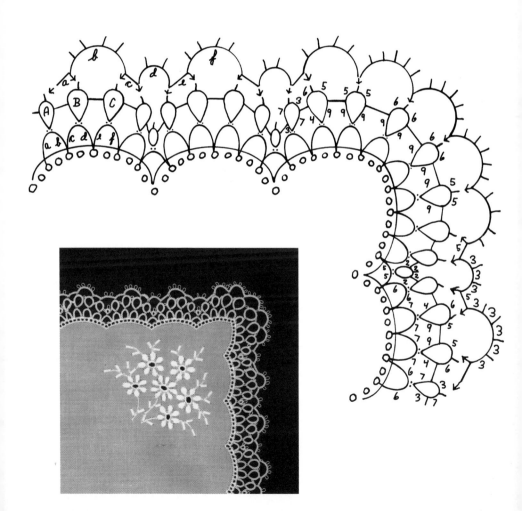

Lace No. 7

2 shuttles.
Thread no. 80.
Tatted directly onto the handkerchief in one round.
Do not forget to the exchange shuttles at ~.

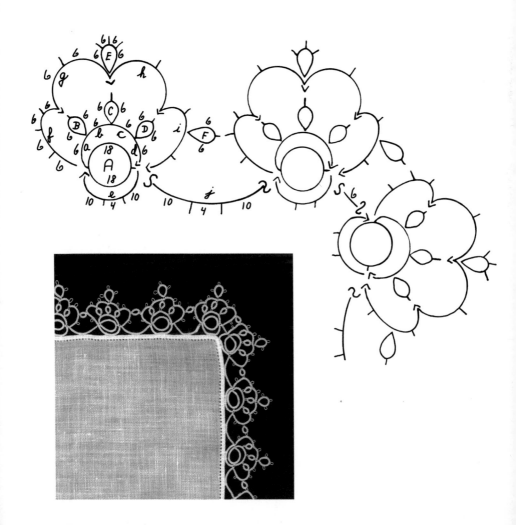

Lace No. 8

2 shuttles.
Thread no. 80.
Tatted directly onto the handkerchief in 2 rounds.

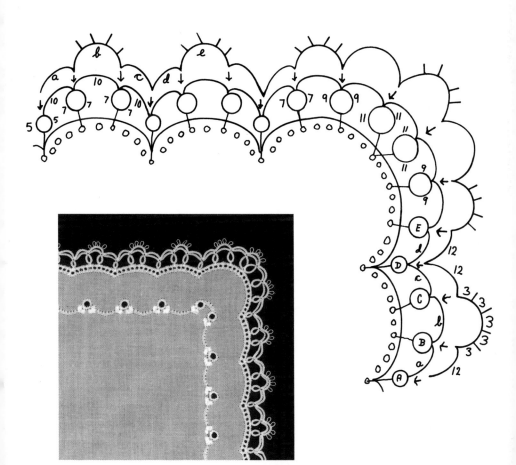

Lace No. 9

2 shuttles.
Thread no. 60.
Tatted in one round. Do not forget to exchange shuttles at ~.
Sew the lace to a piece of fine linen with a hemstitch.

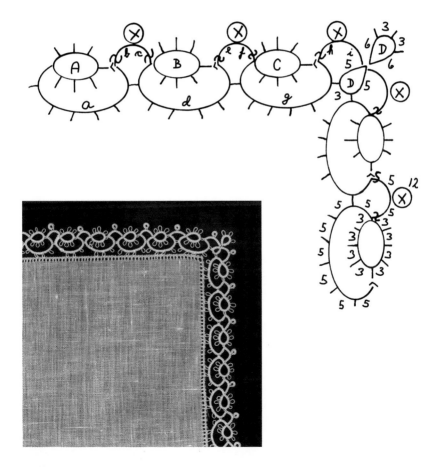

Lace No. 10

2 shuttles. Thread no. 80.

Tatted in one round. When chain a is tatted a paper clip is placed around the thread of shuttle 1 before the chain b is tatted. Chain c is joined to the created space.

Do not forget to exchange shuttles at ~ in the corners.

Sew the lace to a piece of fine linen with a hemstitch.

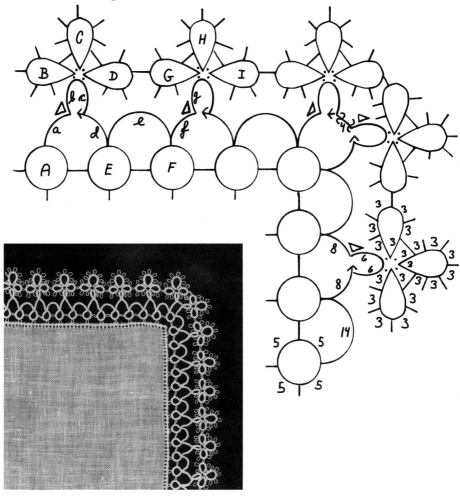

Lace No. 11

2 shuttles.
Thread no. 80.
Tatted in 2 rounds.
The long picots between each motif in the outer round are twisted twice.
Sew the lace to a piece of fine linen with a hemstitch.

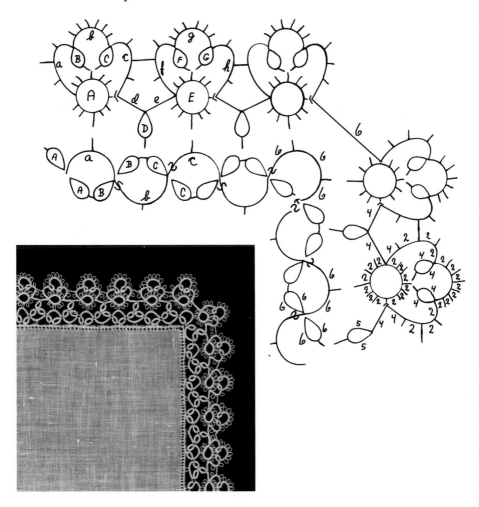

Lace No. 12

2 shuttles.

Thread no. 60.

Tatted in one round.

Sew the lace to a piece of fine linen with a hemstitch.

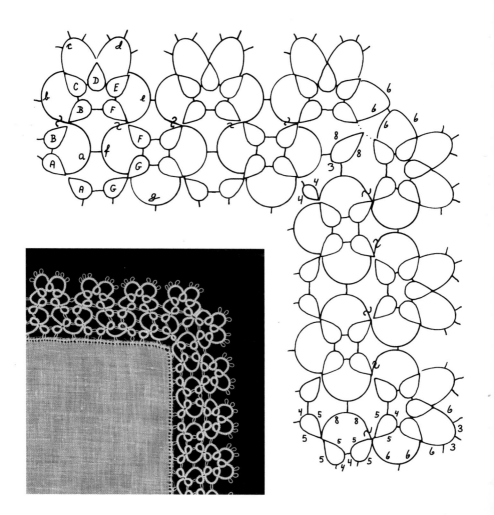

How to work hemstitch

Pull 2 threads out of the fabric where the hemstitch is to be worked.

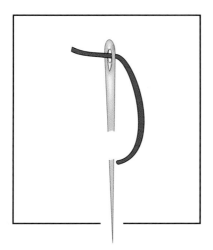

Figure 1: Sew around 3 threads from the pulled section.

Figure 2: Sew around 3 threads in in the fabric and through the picot.

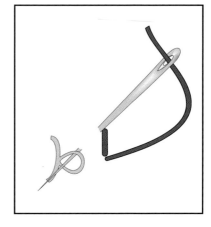

Figure 3: Repeat the sewing through the picot.

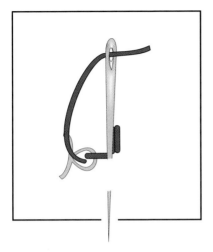

Figure 4: Sew around 3 threads from the pulled section.

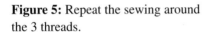

Figure 5: Repeat the sewing around the 3 threads.

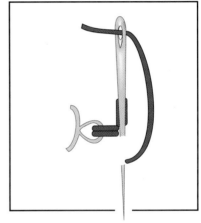

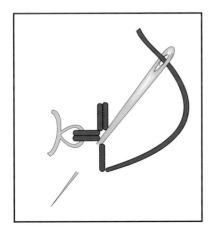

Figure 6: Sew around 3 threads in the fabric.

How to work blanket stitches

Tack the lace onto the fabric.

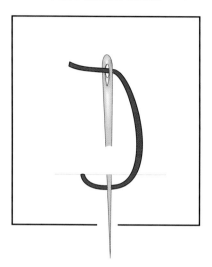

Figure 1: Sew up through the fabric at the basic line of the stitch. Sew a vertical stitch from upwards and down as large as you want the blanket stitch to be.

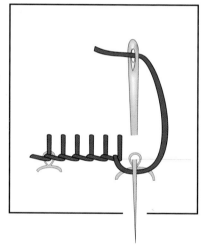

Figure 2: Blanket stitches have to lay closely together.
The lace is joined at the picots as illustrated.

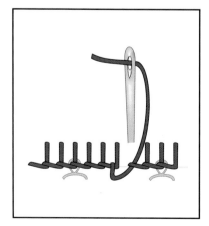

Figure 3: At the conclusion all the blanket stitches are joined by pulling the thread under the thread of the first stitch and slipping the needle down at the top of the row of stitches. Fasten the thread at the backside of the fabric.